Wacky Kid Jokes

Jovial Bob Stine

illustrated by Don Orehek

SCHOLASTIC INC.
New York Toronto London Auckland Sydney

ISBN 0-590-41399-6

Copyright © 1988 by Robert L. Stine. All rights reserved. Published by Scholastic Inc.

24 23 22 21 20 19 18 17   3/9

Printed in the U.S.A.   01

First Scholastic printing, June 1988

JUST BETWEEN FRIENDS

Bob: Go look in the cage over there. You'll see a ten-foot snake.
Matty: Don't try to kid me. I know snakes don't have feet.

Jenny: They're not going to grow bananas any longer.
Bill: Why not?
Jenny: Because they're long enough already!

A couple of friends were sitting on a street corner, fishing into a bucket and looking very forlorn. A kindhearted woman came over and gave them a quarter.

"How many have you caught today?" she asked.

"You're the seventh!" they told her.

Mark: Yesterday I saw a man at school with very long arms. Every time he went up the stairs, he stepped on them.

Jim: Wow! He stepped on his arms?

Mark: No, on the stairs.

Brenda: Hey, you put too many stamps on that letter.

Michelle: Uh-oh. I hope it doesn't go too far now!

John: Are you superstitious?
Kim: No.
John: Then lend me thirteen
 dollars!

Janet: Do you write with your
 right hand or your left hand?
Craig: My right hand.
Janet: That's funny. I usually use
 a pencil.

Emmy: Can I share your sled?
Mike: Sure, we'll go half and half.
Emmy: Thanks.
Mike: I'll have it for downhill, and you can have it for uphill.

Greg: Which is correct — the white of the eggs *is* yellow or the white of the eggs *are* yellow?

Betsy: I don't know.

Greg: Me neither. How can the white of the eggs be yellow?

Eric: Yesterday I saw a man fall off an eighty-foot ladder.

Peter: Gosh, was he hurt?

Eric: No. He fell off the bottom rung.

Jean: Hey, who gave you that black eye?

Gordon: Nobody gave it to me. I had to fight for it!

Louise: Well, how did your clothes get all torn up?

Scott: I tried to stop a kid from getting beat up.

Louise: Who?

Scott: Me!

Margaret: Why are you so upset?
Abby: My teacher yelled at me for
   something I didn't do.
Margaret: What was it?
Abby: My homework!

Tracy: Sometimes I don't think you listen to a word I say.

Matthew: What?

Lili: Do the buses run on time?

Laurie: Yeah. I guess so.

Lili: No — they run on wheels!

Hope: Which is farther away —
New York City or the moon?

Andy: New York City.

Hope: Why do you say that?

Andy: I can see the moon, but I
can't see New York City!

Peggy: Which candles burn longer
— wax candles or tallow candles?

Ron: I don't know. Which?

Peggy: Neither. They both burn
shorter!

YOU'VE GOT TO BE KIDDING!

Tim: Why are you staring at the mirror and standing on your head?

Patty: I want to see what I'd look like if I lived on the other side of the world.

Beth: Why are you staring at the mirror with your eyes shut?

Alice: I want to see what I look like when I'm asleep!

David: Why are you staring at the mirror and jumping up and down like that?

Sally: I want to see what I'll look like when I'm taller.

Phoebe: Hey — there were sixteen cookies left in the cookie jar. Now there are only two. How do you explain that?

Bob: I don't know. I thought I had gotten them all!

Eileen: Why are baby girls dressed in pink and baby boys dressed in blue?

Dan: I don't know. Why?

Eileen: Because they can't dress themselves!

Kevin: What a terrible circus. The knife thrower was the worst!

Anne: Why do you say that? I thought he was great.

Kevin: How could he be great? He threw all those knives at that girl and didn't hit her once!

Cathy: Why are you wolfing down those cookies?

John: I want to eat as many as I can before I lose my appetite!

Craig: Would you help me with my math homework?

Diane: No. It wouldn't be right.

Craig: I *know* that. But at least you could try!

Molly: Did you know that an elephant never forgets?

Steven: Big deal! What has he got to remember?

Katie: Ants are so smart.

Ellen: Why do you say that?

Katie: They always seem to know when we're having a picnic!

Sam: Why did you let the air out of the tires on your new bike?
Mary: So I can reach the pedals!

Alex: What did George Washington, Abraham Lincoln, and Christopher Columbus have in common?

Clark: I don't know. What?

Alex: They were all born on holidays!

Elizabeth: I know how to tell the time at any time of the year by looking at the sun.

Jane: Big deal. I know how to tell the time at any hour of the night.

Elizabeth: How?

Jane: I get up and look at the clock!

Pam: How do you spell Lincoln?
Mike: The man or the car?

Susan: I hope the rain keeps up.
Peter: Why?
Susan: So it won't come down!

Robert: Have you seen my henway? I can't find my henway.

Sue: What's a henway?

Robert: About five pounds! Ha ha! Gotcha that time!

Carol: Why did the rooster cross the road?

Bud: Why?

Carol: To prove he wasn't chicken!

Laurie: Our dog is lost!
Steve: Oh no! You'd better put an ad in the paper.
Laurie: What for? He can't read!

Amy: If your neighbor's rooster comes onto your property and lays an egg in your garden, who owns the egg?

Fred: Gee, I don't know. Who?

Amy: Nobody. Roosters can't lay eggs.

ALL IN THE FAMILY

Sue: Try some of my sponge cake, Dad.

Father: Umm, it's a bit tough, Susie.

Sue: I don't understand why. I made it with a really fresh sponge!

Mother: Why aren't you eating
your dinner?
Jim: I'm waiting for the mustard
to cool off!

Friend: Is that your brother?
Sister: Yes.
Friend: He's very short, isn't he?
Sister: Well, he's only my half
brother!

A brother and sister had a fight and were sent to bed without any dinner. After lying in bed for about ten minutes, the brother decided to make up. So he tiptoed down the hall to his sister's room, and whispered, "Are you awake?"

"I'm not telling you!" she whispered back.

Sister: Why haven't you changed
the water in the goldfish bowl?
Brother: They haven't finished
what's in there yet!

Sister: Mom asked me to fix your grapefruit for you. How much sugar do you want on it?
Brother: Too much, please.

Brother: Dad says we can go to the carnival on Thursday.
Sister: But it's supposed to rain on Thursday.
Brother: Well, if it rains we'll go the day before.

Sister: Where are you going? Mom said not to walk on the kitchen floor unless your feet are clean.

Brother: My feet are clean. It's only my shoes that are dirty!

Sister: Mom just cleaned your room. She says you're not fit to live with pigs.

Brother: Oh yeah? And what did you say?

Sister: I stuck up for you. I said you were!

Sister: Aw, you're a baby. You're afraid to go upstairs in the dark by yourself!

Brother: I am not!

Sister: Yes, you are. Fraidy cat! Fraidy cat!

Brother: I am not afraid. You come up with me and see!

Sister: Uh-oh. Dad's really going to be mad when he sees the big hole you dug in the front yard. What are you going to do with all that dirt?

Brother: Don't worry about it. I'm going to dig another big hole and bury it all!

Brother: Do you know what I'm going to give Mom for her birthday? A beautiful cut-glass flower vase.

Sister: But she already has a beautiful cut-glass flower vase.

Brother: No, she doesn't. I just dropped it!

Sister: Did you tell Mom you broke the vase?

Brother: Yes. I said, "Mom, do you remember that vase you always worried that I would break?" And she said, "Yes, what about it?" And I said, "Your worries are over!"

Sister: Mom wants you to come in and help fix dinner.
Brother: Why? Is it broken?

Sister: Why is it you get into more trouble than anyone else in the family?
Brother: I guess it's because I get up first!

Sister: Mom and Dad just bought me a bird for a pet.

Brother: What kind of bird?

Sister: A keet.

Brother: Don't you mean a parakeet?

Sister: No. They just bought me one.

Sister: Did you clean that fish before you put it in the frying pan?

Brother: Why should I clean it? It couldn't get dirty in the water!

Sister: Well, what kind of fish is it?

Brother: Smelt.

Sister: I know it did. But what kind of fish is it?

Sister: Mom asked you to put salt in the salt shaker. Why didn't you do it?

Brother: I tried, but I couldn't get the salt through those tiny holes!

Sister: What's the matter with you? Mom told you to watch when the soup boils!

Brother: I did! It boiled at exactly 6:25!

Sister: Well, how did you do on that math test yesterday?

Brother: I only got one problem wrong.

Sister: That's great! How many problems were there?

Brother: Twenty.

Sister: So you got nineteen out of twenty right?

Brother: No. I couldn't do the other nineteen!

MAD MUSIC

Richard: Was that you singing as I came in?

Fran: Yes. I was killing time before my singing lesson.

Richard: Well, you're sure using the right weapon.

Frank: I wish you'd only sing Christmas carols.

Megan: Why?

Frank: Because then you'd only have to sing once a year!

April: Well, where's your new guitar?

John: Oh, I had to throw it away.

April: You threw it away? Why?

John: It had a hole in the middle!

Sister: Well, how are you doing with that electronic drum set you got for Christmas?

Brother: Great. It's the most wonderful present I ever got.

Sister: Why's that?

Brother: Dad pays me two dollars a week not to play it!

Chris: How are your violin lessons going?

Liz: Very well. I've already mastered the first steps.

Chris: I thought you were supposed to play the violin with your hands!

Tom: I wish you'd sing solo.

Laura: Solo?

Tom: So low I couldn't hear you! Ha ha!

Laura: Not funny! Have you ever heard yourself sing? You should sing tenor.

Tom: Tenor?

Laura: Ten or twelve miles away!

Lucy: Don't you think my voice has improved?

Holly: Yes, it's improved. But it's not cured yet!

WHAT ARE BROTHERS AND SISTERS?

Brothers and sisters are . . .

The ones you're always tripping over when you're trying to do your homework, and the ones who can't be found anywhere when you feel like a game of catch!

The ones who think it's hilarious to pick up the phone extension and hiccup while you're talking to a friend!

53

Brothers and sisters are ...

The ones who borrow your best white sweater, and when they return it, it's your best *black* sweater!

Brothers and sisters are . . .

The ones who can't explain how
peanut butter got in your
hairbrush!

The ones who can't explain how
your hairbrush got into their room.

The ones who keep their rooms
clean and as neat as a pin because
they spend all their time in yours!

Brothers and sisters are . . .

The ones who think it's fun to tease you all day long about your new haircut. Then when you tease them back, they cry!

The ones you have to find a bathroom for when there isn't a bathroom within twenty miles!

The ones who somehow can't find anything else to do but sit next to you when your friends come over!

Brothers and sisters are ...

The ones who have no idea how all those grasshoppers got under your pillow!

Brothers and sisters are . . .

The ones who, whenever your friends come over, think it's a riot to call you by your totally embarrassing middle name.

The ones who eat the last slice of chocolate cake when you've had your eye on it for hours!

The ones who save their allowance until it adds up to a fortune, while you've spent every penny you ever had!

Brothers and sisters are ...

The ones who magically become
invisible when someone has to walk
the dog on a rainy day.

Brothers and sisters are . . .

The ones who *don't* get caught making silly faces at the dinner table!

The ones who always know how to make you laugh when you're drinking so that you get a quart of milk up your nose!

The ones who want to watch reruns of *Gilligan's Island* when you want to watch the baseball play-offs.

MORE
KIDDING AROUND

Ray: The hissing snakes slithered
in the grass. How many s's in
that?
Bob: Uh . . . seven?
Ray: No. There aren't any s's in
THAT!

Steve: What's five Q plus five Q?
Connie: Ten Q.
Steve: You're welcome!

Brother: Why are you taking that ruler to bed with you?
Sister: I want to see how long I sleep!

Carl: Gee, it's dark out tonight, isn't it?

Christy: I don't know. I can't see.

Shelley: How many famous people were born in Detroit?

Martin: I don't know. How many?

Shelley: None — only babies!

Julie: Why are you running?

Ben: I'm trying to stop a fight.

Julie: Between whom?

Ben: Between me and the guy who's chasing me!

Gary: Earlier today I caught a
jellyfish.
Sarah: Really? What flavor?

Polly: Why do you keep doing the
backstroke?
Robin: I just had lunch and I don't
want to swim on a full stomach.

Mother: Why are you taking that hammer to bed?
Bob: I want to hit the hay!

Sister: Why did you put that lamp in your bed?
Brother: I'm a light sleeper!

Paul: A man who was seven feet tall and fifty inches wide worked behind the counter at a candy store. What did he weigh?

Doug: I don't know. What?

Paul: Candy.

Sister: What are you giving Mom
and Dad for Christmas?
Brother: A list of everything I
want!

Mary: How did you do with the test questions?

Ed: I did fine with the questions. It's the answers I had trouble with.

Ellen: What's worse than finding a worm in your apple?

Joe: What?

Ellen: Finding half a worm in your apple!

Charles: Do you know how to make a fisherman's net?
Jane: Sure. It's easy. You just sew a whole bunch of holes together!

Amy: Do you know what an echo is?
Jeff: Could you repeat the question?

George: Look! I just found a lost football.

Louis: How do you know it's lost?

George: Because the kids down the street are still looking for it!

Brother: Why did Mom give us this for lunch? I hate cheese with holes.
Sister: Just eat the cheese and leave the holes on the side of your plate!

Sister: Haven't you finished that alphabet soup yet?
Brother: Not yet. I'm only up to the K's.

WHY IT'S GREAT TO HAVE BROTHERS AND SISTERS

It's great to have brothers and sisters because . . .

There's always someone around to blame for starting all the fights!

You're not the only one who won't eat the cauliflower!

It's great to have brothers and sisters because . . .

When you catch a cold or the flu, there's someone to share it with!

There are more birthdays to celebrate, and more presents that your brothers and sisters will be delighted to share with you!

There's always someone around who can keep a secret from your mother — at least until she gets home from the store!

It's great to have brothers and sisters because . . .

Your room is not the only one in the house that looks as if it was in the path of a hurricane!

It's great to have brothers and sisters because . . .

There's always someone dying to tell you the end of the movie you're about to see so you don't have to waste your time being surprised!

There's always someone around to help you develop a sense of humor about yourself by teasing you all the time.

There's always someone else in the house who votes for watching *The Monkees* instead of the six-o'clock news, so your dad is outvoted again!

It's great to have brothers and sisters because . . .

There's someone else who will break your best toys so you don't have to feel bad that you did it yourself!

There are always interesting phone conversations to pretend you're not listening to!

There's someone to gobble up all the cookies and candy in the house before you can get to them so you don't have to worry about your teeth rotting!

It's great to have brothers and sisters because . . .

When Mom and Dad are yelling, it isn't always about YOU!

You're not the only one who won't eat liver!

There's always someone around to fight with so you don't have to fight with your friends!

FIFTEEN THINGS A BROTHER OR SISTER WILL *NEVER* SAY TO YOU!

1) "Can I help you clean your room?"

2) "*You* decide what movie we go to. You have much better taste!"

3) "I don't like hanging around with your friends. They're much too sophisticated for me."

4) "Can I finish your lima beans?"

5) "Here's your sweater back. I had it cleaned before I returned it."

6) "You don't have to entertain me while Mom and Dad are out. I'll go up to my room and read a book by myself."

7) "*You* take the biggest piece of pie. I'm too full!"

8) "I'll be happy to lend you ten dollars. Pay it back whenever you can."

9) "Can I do your math homework for you tonight? I don't have much to do."

10) "It wasn't your fault. It was all *my* fault!"

11) "I saw you were on the phone, so I decided to be silent."

12) "Why don't you wear my new Springsteen sweatshirt? It looks better on you!"

13) "Betcha I can wash and dry the supper dishes all by myself!"

14) "*You* sit in the front seat."

15) "*I* started the fight. You didn't!"

LAST LAUGHS

Barbara: Did you hear about the
  boy who keeps going around
  saying no?
Nick: No.

Peter: Why do they call that
  animal a rhinoceros?
Dana: Because it looks like a
  rhinoceros!

Sharon: Hey, your baseball cap is on backward.

Mark: Mind your own business. How do you know which way I'm going?

Pam: Why were you so late for school this morning?

Tim: I dreamed I was playing football, and the game went into overtime!

Bruce: Do you know where I can buy some parrot seed?

Linda: Why? You don't own a parrot.

Bruce: I know, but I want to grow one!

Walter: Did you know that boys are smarter than girls?

Alison: No. I never knew that.

Walter: See what I mean?

Melanie: Did you know that all buses and trains are stopping today?

John: No. Why's that?

Melanie: To let the passengers off!

May: Stop making faces at that
poor bulldog.
Tony: Well, he started it!

Jason: Are you going to the baseball game with me this afternoon?

Emily: No. It's a waste of time. I can tell you the score before the game starts.

Jason: Oh yeah? What is it then?

Emily: Nothing to nothing!

Libby: How was the movie?

Brian: A real turkey. I could hardly sit through it the second time!

Leslie: Hey, what are you doing up in that tree?

Anne: The sign says keep off the grass!

Ken: I'm glad I wasn't born in France.

Debby: Why?

Ken: Because I can't speak French!

Debby: I'm glad I wasn't born in Spain.

Ken: Why? Because you don't speak Spanish?

Debby: That's right! How'd you guess?

Ken: I'm glad I wasn't born in Urehatt.

Debby: Urehatt?! Where's Urehatt?

Ken: It's on my head! Ha ha! Gotcha that time!